A shirt for a party

Story written by Karra McFarlane
Illustrated by Tim Archbold

Speed Sounds

Consonants

Ask your child to say the sounds (not the letter names) clearly and quickly, in and out of order. Make sure he or she does not add 'uh' to the end of the sounds, e.g. 'f' not 'fuh'.

Each box contains one sound. Focus sounds for this story are circled.

f	l	m	n	r	s	v	z	sh	th	ng
ff	ll	mm	nn	rr	ss	ve	zz			nk
ph	**le**	mb	kn	wr	se		se			
			gn		**c**		s			
					ce					

b	c	d	g	h	j	p	qu	t	w	x	y	ch
bb	k	dd	gg		g	pp		tt	**wh**			**tch**
	ck		gu		ge							
					dge							

Vowels

Ask your child to say the sounds in and out of order.

a	e ea	i	o	u	ay	ee y	igh i	ow o
at	h**e**n	**i**n	**o**n	**u**p	d**ay**	s**ee**	h**igh**	bl**ow**

oo	oo	ar	or oor ore	air	ir	ou	oy oi
z**oo**	l**oo**k	c**ar**	f**or**	f**air**	wh**ir**l	sh**ou**t	b**oy**

Story Green Words

For each word ask your child to read the separate sounds, e.g. 'b-u-s', 'p-oo-l' and then blend sounds together to make the word, e.g. 'bus', 'pool'. Sometimes one sound is represented by more than one letter, e.g. 'th', 'oo'. These are underlined.

sort stiff third smart bright boy like

Ask your child to say the syllables and then read the whole word.

birth|day be|fore T-|shirt pa|rrots par|ty danc|ing

per|fect a|round

Ask your child to read the root first and then the whole word with the suffix.

whirl → whirling scratch → scratchy twirl → twirling

squirm → squirmed wriggle → wriggled sleeve → sleeves

itch → itchy sigh → sighed wool → woolly

Vocabulary Check

Tell your child the meaning of each word in the context of the story.

	definition:	**sentence:**
stomped	*walked angrily*	*I stomped around stiffly to show him the way I felt.*
squirmed	*moved around uncomfortably*	*I wriggled and squirmed to show him the way I felt.*
protested	*argued*	*"Dad, it's sparkly!" I protested.*
whirling and twirling	*spinning around*	*Let's do some whirling and twirling.*

Red Words

Red words don't sound like they look. Ask your child to read the words but if he or she gets stuck read the word to your child.

my	would	school	other
some	are	ball	does
one	could	put	what
was	said	would	want
two	water	she	are

A shirt for a party

Do not read the story to your child first. Point to the words as your child reads. If your child gets stuck on a word help him or her say the sounds and blend them together. Re-read each sentence to your child to help him or her remember what he or she has read. Discuss what is happening on each page.

It was the week before Mum's birthday party.

"You will need to be smart for Mum's big day," Dad said. "What you need is a shirt. A smart shirt."

"Dad, no, no!" I said. "Not a shirt!"

"Well let's go shopping and see," said Dad.

In the first shop…

“Go on,” Dad said, “put this shirt on. I like this one.”
But I didn’t like it.
“Dad, the sleeves are too tight,” I said.
“It’s too stiff… I just look silly!”

I stomped around stiffly to show him the way I felt.

In the second shop…

“Go on,” Dad said, “put this shirt on, it’s cool.”
“Dad, it’s not cool,” I said. “It’s itchy. It’s scratchy. It’s woolly!”

I wriggled and squirmed to show him the way I felt.

In the third shop…

"Go on," Dad said, "give this one a go. This is a party shirt. This is perfect."
"Perfect? Dad, it's sparkly!" I protested.
"I will *not* put on a sparkly shirt!"

I crossed my arms to show him I wasn't happy.

In the last shop…

"What sort of shirt do you want?" sighed Dad.

"Hmmm." I said. "Let me see.
It must be soft… it must be bright… it must be…
This one! This is the one! This T-shirt!" I yelled.
"It's got birds on – lots of bright parrots.
Let me have this one, Dad!"

It's party day!

Abdul is first at the door (a boy from school).
"Cool T-shirt," he says.
Emma is second (the girl from next door).
"Good T-shirt," she says.
Uncle Ted is third.
"Smart T-shirt," he grins.

You see, Dad.
I know what's cool.

Let's have fun.
Let's do some dancing.
Let's do some whirling and twirling.

Happy birthday Mum!

Now ask your child to re-read the story helping him or her think about the best way to read each sentence.

Questions to talk about

Read the questions aloud to your child and ask him or her to find the answers on the relevant pages. Do not ask your child to read the questions – the words are harder than he or she can read at the moment.

p.9 Why did the boy need a new shirt?

p.10 The boy didn't like the shirt in the first shop. Why?

p.11 The boy didn't like the woolly shirt. How did he show this?

p.12 The boy didn't like the sparkly shirt. What did Dad think?

p.13 Which shirt did the boy choose?

p.14 What did the people say about the boy's shirt?

Questions to read and answer

Ask your child to read the questions and find the correct answer in the story.

1. The boy needed a smart shirt for **school / his mum's birthday party / his dad's birthday party**.

2. In the second shop the boy **jumped and hopped / wriggled and squirmed / jumped and wriggled**.

3. The sparkly shirt was in the **first / second / third** shop.

4. The T-shirt that the boy picked had **parrots / dogs / fish** on it.

5. **Abdul / Mum / Uncle Ted** was first at the door.

Speedy Green Words

Ask your child to read the words clearly and quickly – across the rows, down the columns, and in and out of order.

happy	door	day	know
good	birds	week	shirt
party	look	will	see
day	for	show	door
too	felt	birds	girl